Vintage
95

LEAGUE OF CANADIAN POETS

National Poetry Contest

Over 17,000 poems have been entered in the League of Canadian Poets' National Poetry Contest since it began in 1987. These poems have shown the vitality and diversity range poetry community is in this country. The National Poetry Contest is the largest competition in Canada. The top 50 poems are gathered into an anthology each year. From these poems, the top three are chosen and cash prizes of $1,000, $750 and $500 are awarded.

Poems entered in the contest are unpublished and no longer than 75 lines. All entries must be typed, single-sided on plain 8 1/2" x 11" paper. As the contest is judged blind by a jury of poets, the author's name must not appear on the poem, but be submitted on separate sheet, along with an address and phone number and the titles of all poems entered. Copyright remains with the poet, but winners are asked to allow for the first rights to print their work.

There is an entry fee for each poem and payment, either by cheque or money order in Canadian funds, should be included with the submissions. Deadline for the entries is January 31st of each year. Winners are announced at the LCP's Annual General Meeting.

Since the competition's inception, the winners have been:

1988 1st poem: Michael Redhill
     2nd poem: Sharon Thesen
     3rd poem: Cornelia Hoogland

1989 1st poem: Elisabeth Harvor
     tied: Elyse Yates St. George
     tied: Patricia Young

1990 1st poem: Diana Brebner
     2nd poem: Blaine Marchand
     3rd poem: D.J. Eastwood

1991 1st poem: Elisabeth Harvor
     2nd poem: David Margoshes
     3rd poem: Debbie Fersht

1992 1st poem: Nadine McInnis
     2nd poem: Stan Rogal
     3rd poem: Louise B. Halfe

1993 1st poem: Joy Kirstin
     2nd poem: Patricia Young
     3rd poem: Gabrielle Guenther

1994 1st poem: Tim Bowling
     2nd poem: John Pass
     3rd poem: Sue McLeod

1995 1st poem: Catherine Greenwood
     2nd poem: Sophia Kaszuba
     3rd poem: Neile Graham

For more information, please contact the League of Canadian Poets, 54 Wolseley Street, 3rd floor, Toronto, Ontario, M5T 1A5, tel.: (416) 504-1657.

Vintage 95

L E A G U E   O F
C A N A D I A N   P O E T S

National Poetry Contest

Edited by Linda Rogers

QUARRY PRESS

The publisher acknowledges the support of
The Canada Council, Ontario Arts Council,
and Department of Canadian Heritage.

Canadian Cataloguing in Publication Data

   Vintage 95, the League of Canadian Poets

Poems by winners of the national poetry contest
   sponsored by the League of Canadian Poets.
ISBN 1–55082–170–9

   1. Canadian poetry (English)--20th century.

I. Rogers, Linda II. League of Canadian Poets.

PS8279.V56 1996   C811'.5408   C96-900399-4
PR9195.25.V56 1996

Cover art by bill bissett,
reproduced by permission from the artist.

Design Consultant: Keith Abraham.
Typeset by Larry Harris.
Printed and bound in Canada by Essence Publishing,
Belleville, Ontario.

Published by **Quarry Press Inc.**,
P.O. Box 1061, Kingston, Ontario K7L 4Y5.

Eighth National Poetry Contest
PRIZE WINNERS

First Prize
Catherine Greenwood
"The Stillbirth"

Second Prize
Sophia Kaszuba
"The Bruce Peninsula"

Third Prize
Neile Graham
"On Skye"

Contents

Preface

I like the nearly new Vintage title for the National Poetry Contest anthology. It suggests a tasting, sips from silver chalices, which takes us back to our ritual beginnings.

Poetry is a community experience. As we all sit round the table with our vintage wine and our poems, what we taste becomes more than wine and poetry. "L'elixir d'amour," ambrosia, mouthwash, vinegar, a sacrament. We argued about that, sniffing, sloshing, and swallowing a lot of words.

The table this year was expanded because of the large number of submissions. Four tasters became six. Patricia Young, Susan Musgrave, Derk Wynand, and I moved over and made room for Cathy Ford and Brian Brett. We didn't even talk about gender parity as we tasted over four thousand poems.

Some years, you have heard, there was a cry of Eureka! The perfect blend of compost and sunlight, perfect poem, perfect agreement. This was not so in 1995. We disagreed, violently. Phones were slammed down. Insults were hurled. One juror, who pushed very hard for a certain poem with an animal in it, was told to go to the S.P.C.A. and adopt one. The jurors were passionate. This is a good thing.

Because we believe poetry is one of the few flavours left in an increasingly bland world, we welcomed our feelings the way you enjoy a slight inebriation. It went to our heads! In the end, we agreed on a shortlist that reflected our pleasure in experiencing the humanity that was their common impetus. Any one of the top or so poems, we felt, could have placed first.

When we chose "Stillbirth" to represent all of them, it was because the poem spoke of the simple aspirations that motivate the human continuum. We are born, we love, we die. Even in death, lives the miracle of birth. There is grace in it and in that grace is hope.

After the decision was made, I spoke to a friend who had taught Catherine Greenwood, the author of the poem. Her delight reminded me there was another aspect to the story of "Stillbirth," that poets are a family that give birth to one another.

The second place poem, "The Bruce Peninsula" by Sophia Kaszuba, has a line that keeps singing in my head. It is "I live big in my apartment trying to get out." Is this not what Michelangelo was saying when he struggled to release the Biblical prophets from marble? It is not the modern condition, as we struggle to maintain our humanity with less and less space in our world and our houses and our heads to do it in?

And then third is Neile Graham's astonishingly beautiful "On Skye," an exquisitely wrought poem that brings the mythology of old worlds into the new even as scones cooked on a fire harden into stones that become the permanent architecture of family.

There are many fine moments in this collection, the representative fifty poems we selected from many that were, by turn, heartbreaking and funny, some of them awesome in their beautiful unreadiness for the world like the calf that dies in the first prize poem.

The energy of this poetry speaks well for us at a time in our civilization when there is a temptation to despair. Plainsong and babble, speaking in tongues — it is dialogue, between ourselves and with the angels who intervene on our behalf. When the going gets tough, the poets get going. Out of the compost of hard times, come some very fine grapes. My father likes to sing this song: "From the vine came the grape. From the grape came the wine. From the wine came the song of a lover." Most of the poems entered in the 1995 contest focused on aspects of love. Love is the grape flavoured ink of the pen that is mightier than the sword.

Linda Rogers
Victoria, January 1996

Notes on the Authors

SYLVIA ADAMS is an Ottawa poet and short story writer and twice winner of Canadian Authors' Association National Capital Region contest for free verse. Her poems have been published in *Arc, Hook and Ladder, Vintage '91*, and several anthologies. Currently she is working on a novel.

AMY BARRATT is a Montreal poet whose work has appeared in *Quarry* and *The Antigonish Review*, among others.

JOHN BARTON lives in Ottawa. His six books include *Notes Toward a Family Tree*, which won the Ottawa-Carleton Book Award, and *Designs from the Interior*, which won the Archibald Lampman Poetry Award.

JACQUELINE BELL is an Edmonton poet whose work has appeared in *blue buffalo, Dandelion, The New Quarterly, Vintage '94* and, most recently, in the anthology *Our Fathers*. In 1995, she was co-winner in the Other Voices Sunday Contest.

MARIANNE BLUGER has written six books of poetry, the latest of which, *Tamarack & Clearcut*, will be co-published by Penumbra and Carleton University Press in 1996. *Summer Grass* (1992) won the Archibald Lampman Poetry Award. She is at work on a collection of tanka as well as a book of lyrics, "The Journal of Albion Daylight." For the record, she once was a Zen Master's wife.

TIM BOWLING is a Fraser River salmon fisher currently on a one-year leave of absence at the University of Alberta in Edmonton. He placed first in the 1994 League of Canadian Poets' National Poetry Contest, and is the author of one book, *Low Water Slack* (Harbour Publishing, 1995).

MARGO BUTTON lives in Nanoose Bay, B.C. She has just finished her first manuscript, *The Unhinging of Wings*, which is about her son who was schizophrenic. She won the Honourable Mention in the 1994 League of Canadian Poets' National Poetry Contest. Her poems have been published in *Fiddlehead, Dalhousie Review, Canadian Literature, Dandelion, Event, CV2*, and other magazines.

ARWYN CARPENTER is 24 and is a graduate of York University's Creative Writing program. She works as a writer, modern dance teacher, and choreographer in Toronto.

ADAM CHILES was born in London, England. He has travelled extensively throughout North and Central America. He is currently wading through his third year of an Honours English degree program at the University of Victoria. His publications include *The Inner Harbour Review, Corridors* (Downtown Press, Montreal). He was shortlisted for the Emerging Poets collection *Breathing Fire*, edited by Patrick Lane and Lorna Crozier. This is his first major publication.

EUGENE COMBS is a Professor Emeritus of Comparative Religions at McMaster University. His publications include *Modernity and Responsibility* (1983), *Genesis and Chandogya Upanisad* (1986), *Runpoem* (1992), *Weeds, Dad Stories* in *The Globe and Mail's* Facts and Arguments column. He won First Prize in the Canadian Authors Association Poetry Contest, 1992.

BARRY DEMPSTER's most recent books are *Letters from a Long Illness With the World, The D.H. Lawrence Poems*, and *The Ascension of Jesse Rapture*, a novel. He is a poetry book review editor for *Poetry Canada*.

SYLVIA J. DORLING lives in Vancouver and is a student of creative writing at the University of British Columbia. She is working on her first manuscript of poems. Her poetry has appeared in *Whetstone*.

PAULETTE DUBÉ of Jasper, Alberta, has received a James Patrick Folinskee Prize in English, the Edmonton Journal 22 Annual literary Award, and Alberta Film and Literary Arts Junior Writers grants. Her poem *Secrets from the Orange Couch* placed first in People's Poetry Award 1994. In 1994 and 1995, she was a finalist in the League of Canadian Poets' National Poetry Contest.

MICHAEL DUDLEY's recent poetry collections include *Returning* (Proof Press) and *Growing Through the Dark* (King's Road Press). His life is blessed by the inspirational presence of his eight-year-old daughter, Regis.

ERIC FOLSOM is a long-time resident of Kingston and author of *Poems For Little Cataraqui* (Broken Jaw Press). He writes book reviews and teaches creative writing. His peanut butter chocolate chips cookies have a growing reputation!

ROBERT GORE lives in Vancouver. His work has appeared in the *Antigonish Review*.

NEILE GRAHAM is a Canadian writer currently living in Seattle, Washington. Her poetry collections include *Seven Robins* and *Spells for Clear Vision*, which was shortlisted for the Pat Lowther Memorial Award for the best book published in 1994 by a Canadian woman.

CATHERINE GREENWOOD is completing a B.A. in English and Writing at the University of Victoria, where she has attended workshops taught by Lorna Crozier. She has had poetry published in *Grain* and *Prism International*. In Victoria, she works for the B.C. Ministry of Health.

GABRIELE GUENTHER's work has appeared in numerous American and Canadian journals, including *Quarry, Malahat Review, Chicago Review, Fiddlehead, Poetry Canada*, and *Prairie Schooner*.

MAUREEN HARRIS is a writer who lives in Toronto. She works one day a week at the bookstore Writers & Co, and does technical writing as well as poetry and essays. She has a book published, *A Possible Landscape* (Brick Books, 1993). These poems are from her second poetry manuscript, "Only The Woman in the Poem."

JAN HASIUK lives in Toronto. It's not California but at least he's not in jail.

GARY HYLAND is a Moose Jaw writer and editor. He is a past finalist in other League of Canadian Poets' National Poetry Contests and the National Magazine Awards, and winner of the poetry manuscript award from the Saskatchewan Writers Guild. His most recent book is *After Atlantis* (Thistledown, 1991).

KEVIN IRIE is a Toronto poet whose work has been published in magazines in Canada and abroad, including *Descant, Quarry, Event,* and *The Kyoto Review.* He appeared in *Vintage 91* and has published a book of poems, *Burning The Dead* (Wolsak & Wynn, 1992).

DAYV JAMES-FRENCH has published widely in periodicals in Canada, the U.S.A., and Australia. A story collection, *Victims of Gravity*, was released by the Porcupine's Quill. He lives in Ottawa.

SOPHIA KASZUBA grew up in northern Ontario and now lives in Toronto. She has published poetry in a number of magazines, including *Arc, Antigonish Review, Dandelion, Descant, Quarry, Poetry Canada,* and *New Quarterly.* She was a finalist in the 1994 League of Canadian Poets' National Poetry Contest.

KATHERINE KERR has a background in art, design, and architecture. She won the second prize in the 1994 Short Grain Prose Poem Competition. She has self-published two chapbooks: *Urns on the Edge* (1993), and *Prairie Poems* (1994), both by Poetik Press.

SABINA KIM lives and goes to a college in Toronto. Most recently she was published in *absinthe* and *Lodestone*, an anthology edited by Ven Begamudré.

ANETTE LEBOX is a poet and fiction writer from Maple Ridge, B.C. Her work has appeared in *Event, Poetry Canada, Grain, Whetstone,* and *The Southern Review.* She is the author of three children's books.

SOPHIA LECKER is a writer and teacher who lives in Ottawa. "They Prayed For No Reason" is the second poem she has had published.

BILLIE LIVINGSTON is from Vancouver but she has been living in Toronto since 1992. Her work has mainly been published in the U.S.A., England, and Australia. She is currently working on a novel for which she has just received an Explorations grant.

ALICE MAJOR is a poet, novelist, and freelance writer living in Edmonton. Her poems have been published and broadcast across Canada, and her first poetry collection, *Time Travels Light*, was published in 1992. Her novel for young readers, *The Chinese Mirror*, won the Fourth Alberta Writing for Youth Competition.

DAVID O'MEARA has had poetry published in *The Antigonish Review* and *TickleAce*. He is currently living in Ottawa.

LOUIE PAZONIA was born in Naples, Italy in 1943. He moved with his family to Vancouver in 1960, where he attended the University of British Columbia. He graduated with a B.A. in English literature. He and his wife Lucille live with their five children in North Vancouver, B.C.

JOHN REIBETANZ has written *Ashbourn* (Véhicule, 1986), *Morningwatch* (Véhicule, 1995), and *Midland Swimmer* (Brick Books, 1996). A finalist in the 1995 National Magazine Awards, he teaches at the University of Toronto.

STAN ROGAL was born in Vancouver and now lives in Toronto. His work has appeared in numerous magazines and anthologies. He has two books of poems and a book of short stories published.

E. RUSSELL SMITH was born in Toronto and educated in Montreal. His poetry chapbook *The Pool* appeared in Cambridge (U.K.) in 1972. *Trippers Tales* (short stories, 1991) and *The Felicity Papers* (novel, 1995) were published by General Store Publishing House. His poems have been seen in many journals across Canada and in the U.K.

CAROLYN MARIE SOUAID lives and writes in Montreal. Her work has appeared in *The Urban Wanderers Reader* (Hochelaga Press, 1995), *Vintage '92*, and several Canadian magazines. This poem is from her current manuscript "Hollow Grass."

ANDREA THOMPSON was born and raised in Toronto, and received her B.A. in psychology and creative writing in Ottawa. Upon graduation she high-tailed it to Vancouver to continue her polymorphic study of language, myth, and form. Publications include *Room of One's Own, Arts Vancouver*, and recently *Euphony* magazine on the Internet.

RUSSELL THORNTON lives in Vancouver and has published poems in various journals, including *Canadian Literature, The Malahat Review,* and *Poetry Canada Review.* He has a collection forthcoming called *The Pathways Through the Apple.*

RHEA TREGEBOV's fourth collection of poetry, *Mapping the Chaos,* was published in 1995 by Véhicule Press.

CHRISTL VERDUYN lives in Peterborough, where she teaches and writes about Canadian literature. Her poetry has appeared in *The Dry Wells of India, Canadian Forum, Canadian Women Studies,* and *Wascana Review.*

SUE WHEELER won the 94/95 Kalamalka New Writers Award for her first manuscript, *Solstice on the Anacortes Ferry*, published in the fall of 1995.

Vintage
95

LEAGUE OF
CANADIAN
POETS

The Stillbirth

Dreaming a different life
my father moved us in the dead of winter
to an abandoned ranch he'd found
in the mountains. The summer before
he'd walked the welcoming land, conceived
a scheme with almanacs and advice that flowed
free as the homemade wine of his neighbours, bemused
ranchers who wondered why a city man would forfeit
his salaried ease. He sat
with them on their evening porches, seeing
the gentle yellow order of the freshly swathed
fields, hearing the random
bleating of calves echo through the hills.

His children would flourish like the wild
alpine flowers that grew there
in spring. In summer he would teach us
the names of grasses — *timothy, clover, oats, wheat.*
In winter we would become strong
hauling hay and water, mucking stalls
in the old wooden barn.

That long January   the only
winter we were there,
as the eldest I helped my father
feed the four Herefords. Our starter herd.
One morning in the early darkness
he found one of them had calved
too soon. He called me to the paddock
where the small body gleamed,
its upper side already leavening.
A smell like yeast rose from the salty
amniotic puddle it lay in.

It was perfect. Grotesque, hairless
except for white fringes on the shut
eyes, mouth and nostrils closed, hooves
still rubbery. Nearby the cow stood quietly
chewing the grain my father gave her, and
as he held her bucket he explained to me
gestation and its failures.

When he dropped me at the schoolbus
that morning my mouth was full of new words,
my ten year old's tongue morbidly savouring
the taste of things gone
wrong. I silently repeated their
magic — *stillborn, aborted, premature,* —
as if they could convey the seamless
unfinished body and blue umbilicus
leaking into the frozen ground, the calf
first born of my father's dream.

The Bruce Peninsula

I

I have money. The kind that goes from the beginning
to the end of the month. I get a bus ticket
and go up to the Bruce. Rain on the window. A baby cries.

In Owen Sound are new malls,
coloured leaves in a school yard.

I go up to the Bruce today.
The old Indian in the land we will never push up
into our blood, stays down in the ground
pushing the soul up with his hands.

Blood is in everything, west love,
wishes, land rights, rights on the lake.
The pink blue light in boys and girls
grows into towns, highways, farms.

I live big in my apartment trying to get out.

II

It's like this with me: deep inside, I want to get out and live.
The pictures jump around like bad TV, like wishes in a store.
When we meet at work we never tell our stories
we work by ourselves. "All by myself,"
says Esther, says Tom.

Up in the Bruce in the old house
is a trunk full of pictures.
The people who built up the farm,
fill the cemeteries all around.

III

I know myself. (I am by myself.)
My heart takes the hands of the sun
and climbs out onto the surface. I get cold
by myself on the surface. I want
the twilight to fill up with people talking.

At work my friends and I don't look out
and I don't look out. We work like a business.
We go home at night to apartments
high in the city of pink light,
we watch TV and eat dinner by the stove.

IV

The Huron Indian waits by the roots of the pine
and calls the stars by name.
The photographs in the trunk lie one on top of the other.
In the empty house live mice and squirrels and bats.

We lie down one on top of another, in the empty house
like photographs in the trunk.

On Skye

Hard to know the right madness here —
Skye's hills have the twisted pine scent
of Montana, the air of Coyote's

bitter-bright games — but here the road
crosses the bridge where Macleod
said goodbye to his faery wife

and leads to the ruins of Trumpan Church
where Clan Macdonald was burned alive
by Clan Macleod. The crofts crumple

like abandoned ranches, houses and barns
folding in on themselves, stones falling
one by one. Here it was not hard weather

that emptied the fields but the Clearances:
the landlords and everywhere their sheep.
Stacks and hills and emptiness. Stones

rearing to the sky: churches and brochs
bending stone by stone nearer the grasses,
castles full of nettles and sheep, weeds

growing right to the sea, and everywhere,
on church walls, sea rocks, corners
of the castle windows, a strange green fern,

bright with brownish stems, everywhere
springing from the cracks in stone.
I dreamt a dog whose hair was these

ferns, thick, rich, alive. Looking at her
I saw how the stones love this land,
how the rain and wind and tides love stone,

how the grass does, how the woman who once lived
in the fallen croft shaped scones
from flour and sang while her children —

who grew to leave for the New World —
woke to the sure rhythm of her work
and the haunting lilt of a piper's tune

reeling in the righteous wind.
All this, with my fingers woven
into fronds on her back, moving from the cool

green growth to the warmth that rose
from her skin. And in the pause of flying home,
right at the Rockies' feet, there she is again:

standing stiff in the wind as my plane
touches down on the runway right by her.
A wolf on the tarmac, the blowing snow

swirling around her feet like fog,
like the cold and deep warmth
of her feral, human breath.

As a stranger: Abuja, 1989

In the days when we still know the comfort of silence
together, we go to Abuja, the city
like beaten gold, our driver drumming the car
through the four-lane, islanded avenues.
A side tour on the way to Kano.
You and I in the back seat, straining to hear
our protector and guide, the professor from Ile Ife.

And there is no one; the streets are empty.
Laid open to conquering armies.
A *Mary Celeste* abandoned by her crew.
A movie set fired for a cast of gods.
Among four towers the domed mosque
crowns this oasis, this fleck of gold
in Nigeria's iris.
A government seat awaiting politicians,
civil servants to curtain the windows
of these rows of pristine houses
where already hedges are clipped
and flower beds tended by phantom hands.

No one, no sign of life. No
lean dogs quarrelling for scraps,
no horses or goats, delivery vans, battered orange buses
floating on heat, windows rolled open like slack mouths,
black limbs lolling. No
calabash players bobbing and weaving for naira
through clusters of tourists.
No mammy-puts with glass-cased akara on their heads.
No slogans on urine-stained walls, scum-green ditches
frothing, baskets of tie-dyed laundry under the bridges.
No river-blind beggars clawing fenders and windshields,
no crippled boy on his stomach under the hotel magnolia,
crying, Momma, Momma, you got something for me?

In the days when we told ourselves stories,
when your skin glowed like the skin of a young man,
and your hair fell across your forehead, rain-silken
and I, I was drunk on colour, dreaming of durbars,
of market stalls walled with cottons — carmine and indigo —
of trays of silverstone, malachite, mille fiori

already the thin grey ribbons of doubt threaded
through all that colour. We hardly
noticed them, forgetting there was a time
when we'd never heard of this place, never written
the script of a dream

to go to Abuja again. To go as a stranger in silver
and gold, to dance in the streets, I in bangles
and long, full skirts, hair swinging loose
on my shoulders; to lie beneath oleander shouting
our songs 'till they echo from Zuma Rock. To be able
to say that no one will know, or laugh, or remember.
Perhaps on the only day in history that no one goes to Abuja.

But how decorous we were, how impassive our driver, how
didactic our fellow passenger, the professor from Ile Ife.
How easy it was to say, it will always be here
to escape to — forgetting that love is nothing more
than a frantic race against time.

                          We are empty now
and it's too late; I can't even remember when
I stopped loving you, can't remember your eyes,
that hollow brightness that should have told me
the years were running out, take what you can,
this photograph, those beads, that flower for pressing,
one translucent amber jar to place in a winter window

to remember Abuja. The dome and its towers tarnish
as the early night swallows the sun,
and we drive on, the professor pointing north.
In Kano, he says, the hotel will have no water,
the desert sand grinds into your bread,
and yellow-breasted kare birds, tiny and shrill,
festoon the trees with their nests, each
rounded basket hanging from its branch
by a single, long, delicate straw.

Family Pictures: Sunday Dinner

Rain and hail battering the windows;
somewhere outside a power line blows down,
cloaking the house in darkness, just as

my mother, with a flourish, produces
a perfect roast from the oven. We
light candles, pull chairs to the table,

and soon she is telling how she lost us
that time, my sister and I, down
in the village; her pale fingers

stirring the air like water, images rising
before us like pictures developing
in a darkroom, pulled into focus by her voice:

Two little girls in matching sundresses
one brown, one blonde head, side-by-side
toddling towards the river;

the strong bones of my mother's face,
younger, her hair swept up in the back;
she steps out of a shop to a sidewalk

that stretches empty
for what seems like miles in both directions,
hoists the heavy baby, my brother,

higher on her hip, and starts to run . . .
And as if we'd never heard any of this before,
As if we didn't know how it all turns out —

my sister right here beside me, pouring
red wine in the candlelight —
everyone at the table leans in

to the sound of my mother's voice
Just then, a shock of lightning, blue-white,
lights up the room like an X-Ray;

like a darkroom door thrown suddenly open,
forces a glimpse of something pale, unfinished,
floating face-down in shallow water.

The Piano

It was something you would never
let me play, the body

of its music never to be drawn
out by my fingers, its keys

tantalizing and just beyond reach.
Sheet music open on its stand,

notes dark as the sheen of its hinged
lid, a rich and luminous eggplant

dozing past twilight in the garden.
You kept it to yourself, this

upright locked in the study,
its body reserved for your touch,

alone with it — a postwar test pilot
in the cockpit of your Phantom

(I was born after the war);
such a night fighter high above us

all, father, high above your family,
speed and ascent scored across

the clouds' wind-shred staff,
such passion, such bruises

invisible against the deepening
indigo sky, your music

camouflaged by the operatic
drone of the engines.

Baby on another woman's carpet

It starts like a taste
at the back of your throat
a hum in fingers
ancient instinct
to touch   hold   grab onto

the baby smells of special shampoo
powder   clothes carefully washed
in gentle detergent
this baby reeks of love

maybe it's that   my hand wants to grasp

all my carefully sounded
arguments for remaining childless   crumbling
like biscuit in her fingers

Senses blaring   a sudden clarion
call to sexuality
the body stirred   summoned   leaving
the mind   to follow   slowly
like a loping   simian   ancestor

The Zen Master's Wife

After years hushing infants so he could sit in silent meditation
years sweeping rage-broken rice bowls
migrainous years cowering by wrecked family antiques
gathering courage to leave

after years of kidnap and murder-threats
nightmare years flailing stick arms at darkness
years of courtroom terror years of shot nerves
of drifting Gauloise smoke when rough coughs
masked gasps or screams or sobs . . .

after years of confused debriefing questions
such as why did he marry: for Lust for Cash
for Immigration but why did you have him

after years turned chaste nun imploring
the Haesychast prayer and just holding on
to that icon in turn with idiot routine work

after years when Only Friend the strike-out pitcher
champion pacifist fox-kit orphan son
of the-almost-governor-of-Texas gave up
his knightly longing and was gone

after years on welfare kibitzing with ghosts
of Daddy's Nazi persecuted past
and Mother's genteelly vicarious biographies
background years static and newsless except
for reports in exotic journals
which always read thus: 'The Master Prospers'

after years telling a man in a room in a chair
what seemed at first like just a novel tale
with the shame of what impulse had done to the children
until one overcast afternoon it came
to head-on collision with the fact that someone
had been literally shoved in a corner and pissed on
(and the terrible hysterical pain that flowed
when the pus of that stinking wound was lanced)

suddenly one summer night

satori arrived with a radio

from my bed I could hear
out in the street
jazz — jarring strains
a discord of strings sawing darkness . . .

that music was

and it stopped

then someone woke
who had not been
asleep

and eyes on their optic stems
rotated . . .

in the void there were stars
fire points burning
blue in the blackness

stigmata of cosmos

and a slight wind rose
which stirred the sultry air

like breath it sighed
through the split bamboo blind
as I watched the bars
of moonlight gently bend

————

(in zen praxis it is customary to write a poem
  on the occasion of attaining insight)

In *Albion Daylight*

Everything went
white over-
overexposed
in the nuclear flash

& these are the words of one felled
who afterwards grown cancerous and confined to bed
found in a stainless-steel hospital cabinet
a copy of *Albion Daylight*

> In that journal & is the hub
>
> and the man loves the woman
> because the woman loves the man . . .
> because love is eternal
> there is no cause
> everything simply proceeds
>
> & in that light
> the pure light of radical thought
> settles on the hawthorn each twig
> ignites and the whole tree lifts
> its thousand orange-hearted
> white candle blooms to the hills
>
> from faroff it's Yahweh's fiery cloud
> signal for reverence obedience fear
> and at last you know
> your boots track holy ground
>
> & in that journal it is always now
> but always soon to be winter
> deep frozen blackness
> when even the steamy-breathed animals sleep . . .

& that darkness breeding terror
awakens what must ever thereafter
be illumined by the present
fires of the unforgotten

& in that book the warning stands written
that I would not nor you
survive the failure of love

there is an entry there under *surrender*
how it is must be total remember
the battle we waged to establish
whose was the more steadfast refusal of happiness
& then how we had to forgive
on this page floats our cabin home
anchorless in air adrift on hazed

blue layers of smoke or mist
which daylight at daybreak shall cleave

& the motes there circulating catch
the sun of molecular imagination
which flashing gift for magnification
cannot ever know boredom

roll the pages with your thumb
that wind softly touching your skin
is the *whoosh* of a deer through bracken

or sunset blazing that glory
train passing through town
and all the flatcars freighted with gold
each bearing one
eternity at a time

that wind gently raising your armhairs
moves where it listeth — I told you
it was breath
speaking holy language

you hear it and laugh
& once you have read what you find
in that journal you change

see how I have become
the one who survived her own death
and it was nothing

October

The eyes of those my mother loves most
shine blue as the wings of the Steller's jays
whose swopping madness in the changing
maple leaves she watches through the dew-
dropped front-room window every morning
now, silent, alone, as cup after cup of forgotten
tea goes cold on the mahogany side-table
I made for her in high school woodshop
the fall of 1979, my own blue eyes even then
fated to love the Elisabethan sonnet more
than the dove-
tail joint.

In the birdfeeder, the hazelnuts
she cracks religiously each night before bed
attract a steady flow of flashing blue from
the morning's high cloud of red leaves, like
a pure syrup tapped by what is still most
beautiful in her, the gentleness that whistles
the red-winged blackbird in from the marsh,
that whistled us home her younger years.

Her younger years. What can I possibly know
of these? Or any? She asks. She shakes her head.
If I walk in upon her sadness now, my blue
eyes wide and reflecting the sun, or if my
brothers do, my sister, even our father waking
from his long, cold dream, and if a flock of jays,
wild at the glass, shrieks through our skin as though
our hearts had finally broken for her, can the colour
or the cry still speak with any power
to her capacity for joy?

Now the days are as short as they will ever be.
The leaves swim down in mist, the jays splash
between them. My mother sees with tired eyes
the unfolding of the morning's perfect wings;
they must mean love to her,
they carry the wonder of her children,
her husband's desire, all the blue that's ever
flown out of the world to feed at her life.

Her life. What can I know?
For every unborn morning's sake
I pray to more than god
her eyes flash blue and fly.

A Man's Grief

After the funeral, he dismantles
the sunroom, and builds a new deck
sealed with tar to keep out winter rains. He buries himself
in *Homes and Gardens*, shifting angles and shapes,
when all I want is a corner
to plant my pain. I think of quitting
this house, desecrated now, grief running down its walls.
With a screeching saw, he removes the
railings, pares them like an apple, and
lets the peeling fall away until
the juicy core of the house is revealed, and reveals
the rose garden and firs laden with cones.
Along the decks, he builds a bench, and
paints it blue-black, like a bruise. An armband
of mourning wrapped around the house, and the house,
he re-paints, even the blood-soaked steps, the steps
where his dead son has lain, his face
the pallour of grey, and the house grey too,
fused with leaden sea and sky.

And you keep on...

We were giggly in the car
stopping at every gas station for chocolate
stocking up for the long streches
where trucks would whiz past
and aim dust in Sean's window
and he kept on
waving a cane around
shouting suck it
suck the bobo!

We were giggly too 'cause the night before
Sean kept on drinking Scotch from a coffee cup
with his mother in the kitchen
till she sent him to lie down
on a couch where from my bed
if the door was open
I could see his face
and when he saw mine awake
he tiptoed in to tickle me
till the dogs barked dawn

We were giggly too 'cause
we were leaving the tension of that town
a one brand beer town where after work
the mill men put a two-four in the truck
where sixteen year old Helix fans dragged strollers
where a woman took off her wig to show us its rain damage
where old pals of Sean's it's fair to say
had all hanged themselves

In Managua

The cathedral is empty, they warned me,
but the darkness moves inside, and whispers
from the shadows like barely opened eyes,
watch the heat as it runs down the city,
the vendors are cooking in the square,
and children peel from the hot corners
picking their way through the ruins,
feeling nothing but the grease of fear
crawling in their minds, like animals
biting the air, digesting silence,
they mine the streets with their hands
cupping the sun, as the noon blisters
in Managua, paralysing time, where
the cathedral is haunted by voices
by the sound of children beating
against the dark walls and columns,
its belly aching with the memory
of spirits, the quiet burns
of confession, and the still existing
life in cracks and hiding places,
where the sky drips through the open
windows, the ceiling gaps and holes,
and daylight falls like hot dust
into the chapels throat, like sand
spitting from the sun,
the dark swallows everything,
holding in its rotten breath
the hungry creeps and shuffles,
men that sting the emptiness
with their eyes feeding
desires that suck in the night,
they wait for the shade, as creatures
wait and listen for things approaching,
the cathedral is empty, they warned me,
and yet I feel the nerves itching
as they swarm inside, the wild buzzing
of tongues that lick the air, and taste
my body stepping through the darkness.

41

structure

structure you say   your words like a sudden baton of speech
     striking the anvil deep   inside the orchestral clank of metaphor
our wills sway in proud ethereal fire

you withdraw in flourishes of precipitate grace
     but bring forth measure charged with longing
my brief fate is pinned under fermata   larger than time   gathering enharmonics
     modest modulation   the same notes crossing until we meet

we meet in the subterfuge of dissonance   in the cadence and stress of accord
     i crave the infinite line of crescendo   shy smiles in your eyes avert mine
i am an oblate awaiting the hostias   begging the wafer in your next perhaps

the ensemble constructs nothing less than benedictus
     reeds prolong the sharp embrace of music
there is voice in those swift gestures   an aria of detail in each expression
     our form converts by substance of sound

the sacred cadenza unfolds the drawn curtain   opening mute triads that lift the mass
     we deserve nothing more than simple yes   where once our splendid no stood firm
the chorus of silence affirms each confutatis

chords settle in the clefs of earth   i swear passion finishes in a guess
     or a whisper   or your deft deflections   or a slight twist of the head
i recall the soft dirge of your closing touch even now
     glorious as requiem

lacrimosa divulges slender imperfections of love   next time die slowly
     lingering until i am old with your patterns   until they are resolute
like the trill before sanctus

Chance Encounter

For ten minutes yesterday
I was cosmically loved, not
by some vision of smoke thin wrists
curling from the November mist,
not from a memory blown in my face
like a puff of witch doctor dust, not even
from one of those I-feel-like-the-last-
man-on-earth encounters with God.
No, I was a simple out-of-bounds,
a sticky flurry of sopping leaves, a sudden
leap... one blue eye, one gold, dividing
me into soul and precious body.

If ghosts had tongues like postcoital
penises, then that pounce of wet fur
must have been a four-star phantom.
It looked like Siberian Husky, though
it moved like the Hoover Dam, soaking me
in approval, circling until I was ringed
with afterglow, my jeans streaked with
paw print comets. There was
nothing I could do but open my arms,
like hugging a waterfall, holding nothing back.

Ten minutes of total acceptance: a snout
in my beard, a tail thumping against
my crotch, a quiver of whiskers
melting in my ears. Not a thought
to what diseases we might be sharing.
No need for a Certs or a spurt of cologne.
It took me as I was, excited by the gasp
of my energy, the space in the mist
I'd made for myself, the spot on the street
where my shadow and I folded up into a shield.

Time for one last Siberian lick.
If *Genesis* had taken the trouble
to explain how God made streams,
it would have gone something like this,
a giant tongue and a willing surface.
It certainly felt like the world
was about to begin again, après
flood. I stood there with my arms
outstretched, blissfully embracing
the mist and beyond, as the Angel Husky
bounded off to other chance encounters.

Deer

Amidst the cushy sole prints of Nikes
and the pussy willow pads of pampered
terriers and labs, a sudden set of
deer tracks, a seashell stamp of hooves.
So close to backyard patios, the
chorus lines of marigolds look bruised,
the lawns tousled, a window or two smeared.
In the thick of night, when we're dreaming of
corridors and Dali clocks, the soft brown
bodies of bucks and does are basking
in our moonlight, nibbling on the last of our
lettuce leaves, scratching impressions in our sand.
They are the children we wish we'd had,
fleeting images of ourselves before
inner lives grew blotchy, eyes heavy with
10 p.m. cop shows and those relievedly
nonsensical dreams. They are shadows
of joy and appetite, marauders of
afterglow, property of instinct and whim.

Occasional Fridays or Saturdays
we tiptoe outside at midnight, wishing
we could sneak a smoke or feel up someone
behind the bushes. Longing to be wanton,
even irresponsible. Tear out some
turf, rip a zinnia in two, devour
a handful of fireflies. Although
touching a deer would do, stroking the muscled
satin, drinking from its black coffee eyes.
Leaving a bare footprint next to a pair of
hooves. So, here we are, stroking
the invisible, stamping our feet
through the flowerbeds, fools doing the
Twist or the Frug, the sand between our toes
slowly turning to mud in the dew.

Face it, we no longer belong out here.
Moonlight hurts, like mercury searing
through nerves and tissue. We only have
a minute, calling in the cats, before
we start mistaking every shadow
for something we shouldn't desire.
Slam those doors, snap those chains, curtains keep us
safely 60 watt. How much later is it
before our yards are filled with deer, raccoons,
foxes, unicorns?... we'll never know,
we've already disappeared. Tomorrow,
sun struck, eager to weed or hold a hose,
we'll notice the tracks again, those spilled grains
of sand. *Deer,* we'll whisper, an endearment,
being gentle with our lost, imagined selves.

Castel Ter Sol

In Castel ter Sol, the village
set amidst dry Catalan hills,
where you spend your summers
we always ate late
in the evening when the air
brushed our skin
like the wing of a moth.
The light from the lamp
in the loggia
sought out the shy spirits
that flickered and hid
behind the trees in the garden.
We drank tinto with love
and laughed
until morning

and within the walled garden
the grass lay smooth
and green as the empty
bottle that stood
on the table.
The grass in the fields
beyond the village
crumbled beneath our feet
like the dust of dried sage
when we walked to the farm

(I long to be there
with you again,)
The earth and the sky
crying out for rain.

how i saved my mom

Tits smoked Craven Menthol
and butted them straight down on the fire
Pig smoked Peter Jackson
because he liked the way the unicorn looked
burnt to an ash bubble
Monpy smoked No. 7
and 'pantie packs' of leftovers she found at parties

when they smoked at our place though
we all smoked Sportsman
and used the index finger (no nail marks)
pressing the last of the tube under the filter
into the maple leaf ashtray
so that we wouldn't think
Someone else had smoked in the house

in my daughter's garden

in my daughter's garden
I water the impressions
her hands have made

My Own Ghost

is the bastard who watches over me
        waiting for my life to end

we were looking out the window
        quietly minding our business
    absorbing the frequencies of flowers
        as they rose from the bruised soil
when the phone rang:
    it was the voice of my deceased first wife
    my ghost and I both
            wondered how she found us
        come over right away
           the dead ex- was saying
    I need to talk to you

at that point we woke up
    both of us hyperventilating
    all four hands trembling
my ghost and I asked each other
        whose hands
        whose dreams
        beyond control

the hairs on our chests have been changing
        into creamy white feathers
    wait my ghost keeps saying wait
        this can't happen to me
        I'm a ghost not an angel

we were almost half covered with feathers
    when a strange woman approached us
        as we drew water from the village well

she told us she could read our minds
        my ghost began to mutter
        about not talking to strangers
        but I pointed my thumb at the ghost
            and said him too?
oh yes she said don't worry
            you're not like him at all
            you'll never grow up like him

nevertheless I'm in a trendy bar
        my suede jacket draped over
            a supposedly empty chair on the right
            which in fact my ghost occupies
an older wiser part of my brain, unhaunted
            has been nagging me for days
I'm talking to a guy on my left
            as if I've known him all my life
too hot for imported lager to cool me
            I'm tempering the urge to spill my guts
                as if this guy would care
I'm ignoring my ghost
            making him feel invisible for a change

but the ghost nudges me
        hey he says let's go home
            with somebody tonight
        find someone young and loose
            who likes a ménage à trois
and that older, nagging part of me
        says relax
        switch to scotch
        keep the bar stool warm

shit the ghost says finally
        I've had it I'm leaving
    you want to be alone, fine
        I'm a ghost with self-respect
        and I don't have to sit here
            being ignored by you
he stalks out into the night
        handsome, detestable, elegant
            and completely transparent
            except for a touch of grey hair
    I'm glad to see him go
        one less voice in my head
        one less psychic embarrassment

    hope he's gone for good

Normandy

All the maps of my body
are on fire tonight.

I am confused by history,
caught by the sound
of my father's motorcycle
as he moves across Normandy

and climbs the hill
into the town where I am staying,
the black noise of his engine
shattering the silence in the streets.

In the dark
I wake with the fear of time
and the smell of starched sheets,
the spring night outside expectant,
the air coloured with its own green breath.

When I meet my father in the street
the next morning
I can't believe how young he is,
how his eyes are so blue
they leave me speechless, uncertain

in this town where
all the houses
crowd in on you like gypsies,
they want to tell your fortune,
they want to sell you
something completely unnecessary

and leave you alone
with your ghosts and train schedules
trying to remember
just what it was you came here for.

Walking the Land's Edge, Orkney

History cannot ignore genetics. It is a record of our origins. Our past is a
combination of culture and biology. One without the other is only half of the story.
— Sir Walter Bodmer

The shore is stepped
             with layers of sandstone,
raddled with tide-wrack, rich in the sun.
                     We clamber
up the ledges across the stone plains
rippled by years of waves
             pulling
across its grain. Layers have cracked,
fallen away, bloodred, lava black,
the tan of our skins.
             The green of the hills
just ends, breaks into this wealth of stone
at the edge of the world,
             tumbles down
the crumbling ledge, as though falling here
is what must be done.
             We jump from edge
to edge, west where the ledges march out
to the sea, stone now a pink shading to blue,
blue to green, green to orange
and lichen, kelp.

It's the Ring of Brodgar — thirty stones
tall in the heater
                           between the lochs.
It's the cathedral in the city
and the cobblestones
                              for the sea-town's streets.
It's the weathered slabs
in the graveyard and those carved in
symbols whose meanings we've forgotten
in our own seachange.

It's the tombs and cairns
that range along these hills where we treasured
our parent's bones.
                              Each bay we round
the colours change, the stone
                                        worn into
a different shape. Here a line
undulates like vertebrae
the earth's back
                           slipping into the waves
and gone, then tide-change
and from under the waves
cloud and darkness
                              are rising.

Somewhere in the middle of June when your hip moves against mine

Far from the televised thunder
of the soccer game rumbling
on the front lines of a million bars,

it was a Saturday afternoon somewhere
in the middle of June, the silence
on the streets so enormous it burned.

How safe all seemed, despite the conviction
nothing could save us but a stein
of beer that'd chill us to the bone

like the brittle high-pitched wail
that yesterday had fled the courtyard
to come to equilibrium

above our heads, hovering there like a spear
while we sat, senses cocked,
assessing its frequency till it died

of its own volition, wrapping its sound around our
shoulders like a cool blue scarf.
We expected nothing of the sort today.

At most, a few words of no consequence
as we waved through what we imagined
was heavy and tired and indiscriminate

as the stoppage of cars below glistening
like wet meat on the shores
of a long arid summer spreading

around us familiar as a compilation of moments
that finally brings evening — in
itself unassuming as the curve of your hip

moving against mine in this space
we occupy in each other's lives.
A space that has the ability to grow hot

or cold but lacks definition
when it gallops toward us like something
programmed to kill.

Bloomdale, Ohio

. . . When I can make
Of ten small words a rope to hang the world!
— Edna St. Vincent Millay

At the intersection of what was
and is, a siren

cuts through a life. My sister
leans into this accident
of sound, puts her mouth
to the blade. She's
always preferred the hard things in life.
Her lover's on her knees in a blue sunset
of fields compelling as summer.
Even from a distance, I can decipher
the direction their words have taken.

I've been tracking this sister for decades. As
it is she owns three long acres
of silence, and a dirt road
that swings by, like a cervine rope,
headed for something larger
but smaller
than the hand she now brings
to me in greeting, holding this moment
in her eyes
till it skids and shatters.

Cleaning Cupboards

I'm wearing the belt buckle you gave me like a talisman
but still I say "Don't touch me!", my body lax
and uneasy, intent on something I haven't recognized.
There is a pasture emptying my head, I'm falling through space,
and I haven't asked you if there's a difference between
departure and drowning. The life I made up is so solid.
How can I be evaporating in the midst of it?

I wish I could walk towards you with flames flaring
from my shoulders. I wish I were rising like the fish
in your dreams, from some green river, sequined, glittering,
as lissome as snakes among the leaning ferns.

There are nineteen glasses, two egg cups, two shot glasses,
a coffee mug and a small bin of measuring cups and spoons
on the shelf I've just cleaned and four more cupboards to go.
It's the end of August and the rain is falling at last
creeping up through the basement drain with its burden
of dirt and old leaves, teasing the laundry heaped on the floor.
All this cleaning and things still grow musty.

Once you said to me "If I left my wife now it would be
to live in a cave". Today I've gotten my words wrong twice,
and still I say "I can't do this!" I don't know
what I'm waiting for, I don't even know
what life I would make up for myself if I could
find the door out of this house. Something
I haven't got words for. What I want.

Looking at Pictures of My Daughters

(for Jessica and Katharine)

I've taken so many pictures of you from behind,
mezmerized first by the way your hair
spiralled around your perfect baby skulls
mirroring snailshell and galaxy, this
new universe I'd fallen into.
Year after year I looked at you looking away.

But here's a picture I'd forgotten:
foggy weather and you stand, backs to me and larger
than I knew, on an apron of rock at
the sea's edge.
I can't see your expressions, I don't
know how you feel, there, where
the waves are dark and larger than life.
There's nothing between ocean and sky and
my fear falling into the picture

Standing behind you I hold my heart tight, not
letting out the fear:
that you will be swept away,
that you will turn and see me, hand
across my mouth, eyes round and terrified and

I want you to be happy.
Standing behind you I don't have to see myself
reflected in your eyes, the three of us so muddled
in my heart I can't skim us apart.
I want to be perfect, better
than my mother. My gaze is
the weight on your shoulders. It stiffens your necks.

Reading(s)

Today I would like to be only the woman in the poem,
the one whose name we don't know, or where she came from.
There's a moment when she raises her head or descends a staircase,
perhaps the moment before she has fallen definitively in love,
and the outlook, her destination, are not indicated.
She is fully present in this poem. At its heart lies desire,
hers for whatever will happen, the poet's for the moment's complicity.
Everything around the woman is clear and intense, urging her towards
what is happening outside the poem. Her foot is raised.
As she begins to step forward she turns her head and

I imagine myself stepping through this poem as if it were a membrane.
I'm standing at the foot of a flight of stairs leading to a door.
If I climb them I will find myself looking into the room where
the poet sits. His head leans over the paper on which he is inscribing
a woman's progress across a room. She has turned her head, smiling,
as she leaves to meet someone who, within a year, will become her lover.
The poet hasn't yet foreseen the outcome of that meeting. I have
imagined his eyes (they are a particular pale blue like winter sky)
lifting to see me framed in this doorway. He is startled. He thought
she had gone. He stands and smiles as he steps towards me and

Outside the poem a woman sits on a streetcar reading, her head
leaning against the window. She reads about a woman leaving
both a room and a man, a smile on her lips, on her way
to meet (though she may not know it) her new lover. Then
she reads another poem about a woman entering a room to find
a man seated at a desk writing, so absorbed in his hand moving
across the paper he doesn't notice her. The woman reading is
restless, the streetcar is noisy, the day is sunny. She looks
up from her book to see dull factories along an almost empty
street. She has forgotten where it was she was going.

1966 mustang classic convertible route 66 mantra

i burn gasoline   therefore i exist
i burn gasoline   therefore i exist
i burn gasoline   therefore i exist
i burn gasoline   therefore i exist
i burn gasoline   therefore i exist
i burn gasoline   therefore i exist
i burn gasoline   therefore i exist
i burn gasoline   therefore i exist
i burn gasoline   therefore i exist
i burn gasoline   therefore i exist
i burn gasoline   therefore i exist
i burn gasoline   therefore i exist
i burn gasoline   therefore i exist
i burn gasoline   therefore i exist
i burn gasoline   therefore i exist
i burn gasoline   therefore i exist
i burn gasoline   therefore i exist
i burn gasoline   therefore i exist
i burn gasoline   therefore i exist
i burn gasoline   therefore i exist
i burn gasoline   therefore i exist
i burn gasoline   therefore i exist
i burn gasoline   therefore i exist
i burn gasoline   therefore i exist
i burn gasoline   therefore i exist
i burn gasoline   therefore i exist
i burn gasoline   therefore i exist
i burn gasoline   therefore i exist
i burn gasoline   therefore i exist
i burn gasoline   therefore i exist
i burn gasoline   therefore i exist
i burn gasoline   therefore i exist
i burn gasoline   therefore i exist
i burn gasoline   therefore i exist

i burn gasoline   therefore i exist
i burn gasoline   therefore i exist
i burn gasoline   therefore i exist
i burn gasoline   therefore i exist
i burn gasoline   therefore i exist
i burn gasoline   therefore i exist
i burn gasoline   therefore i exist
i burn gasoline   therefore i exist
i burn gasoline   therefore i exist

November

Brittle leaves scuttering the street. Streams of chimney smoke blurring into clouds.
Wind grey and sleek lining gutters with snow. Trees bleak, beyond meaning now,
not manic cuneiform, not gestures of disease, not eunuchs grim in the shrill light.

You lean to this. You feel knees spreading to release you. Hands that clasp and knot
your bleeding. You feel your breathing begin, the strange pain fibrous beneath
your scream. You see the grey radiance, the white spaces, the sheen of polished steel.

You feel the topaz talisman. Its pale gleam. You receive drawings of a beast, a sky,
so that you may see all that you are, all that you will be. An amber fog twines along
the water where you must kneel, the river that meanders deep into the hallowed land.

The river becomes a creek freezing. A forgotten tent torn, dreaming of grass, feet, dreaming
of arms, lovers humming. Shreds filling with distance and the wreckage of reeds.
The hermit of the sedge who would have hailed you has retreated to another season.

Sleep is your response. Sleep defeats time. Until something in you spreads its arms, yawns
and conceives spring, even now, and you clamber the slopes steeper and steeper
to celebrate winter's easing. The air cuts deep. You breathe keen flakes of glass.

No thaw. The month moves with you, your cowl. The moon a gleam on the creek's
dark ice. Something wants warmth, something sings fire. You gather willow splinters,
the stems of rushes, leaning stalks of yellow grass. You will please whatever sings.

KEVIN IRIE

The Lindow Man

*(Now on display in the British Museum, The Lindow Man is a 2,000 year old body found
preserved in a peat-bog in England. It is believed he was killed as part of some ritual.)*

Who are you, dragged up
as a Lazarus corpse
from out of the earth,
a tanned leather sack
stuffed with bread and bran,
your final meal,
slightly burnt, they say,
like the body of one come back from Hell
with your bones of charred wood,
and one stray fingernail atop your chest
like the carapace sheath
of a deathwatch beetle,
a spent black shell;
your navel,
a soft bullet wound in the gut.

The hairs of your head,
that overturned bowl,
are shredded strands of unravelled burlap,
the frayed sackcloth worn by a penitent
condemned to death,
and the cord that strangled you
is still at your neck
as rusted twine, a swollen vein,
a hatching worm
escaping its host.

And what of your ears,
those small
rusted
dented padlocks,
how many sounds escaped their hearing
while birds called across the marshes,
or mist trolled softly
above your head while rain hammered
its thin silver nails
into the bog,
sealing you under
for centuries and centuries;
your skin, a soaked garment
refusing to be cleansed by this world,
to be turned into silt,
or ash, or seed,
to rise again as water,
or bread;
the peat set like a cast
around your body,
your sex, a soft blind
eel in the mud.

And what could you ever tell us
of death or rebirth —
once the shovel sliced you
like a guillotine blade,
water dripping off you
like fat from cooked meat —
you, back from a Hell where fire was mud,
Orpheus returned alone from Hades,
your bones retrieved like
a broken lyre,
a shattered flute;
a mute Jonah
delivered back to the light
as your body
was pulled and cut
from the earth
like a tongue from
a silenced mouth.

The Effacement of Children

This is a picture of Christmas
when I was just three:
the drunken Dad;
the shattered tree.

The dampening Mum
holds a jagged fragment
of glass, the cupped
angel-remains of a family
tradition.

        This, of course,
was before the divorce.
Divorce, that kin of
cancer: incised
cells reproduced in kind,
multiplied by *step-* and *half-*.
By blood or by paper now,
everyone is related to me.

It is unsafe to marry.

Here, in a corner
like a print from a thumb
large enough to goose
Miss Liberty,
that blur,
that's me.

One Headlight Busted

Her breasts are a place to come and put his head,
dark curls turned to baby's hair.
How she grew up? In one fast breath,
out of all the places she lived,
Charleroi, Kirkland Lake, Toronto,
in a jumble all at once.
Then Wiarton, and then another breath.
Up the hill on the highway of evergreens
in the pickup truck with one headlight busted
to visit a friend by the lake,
deep in the woods down a dirt road
with bumblebees over the weeds in the ditch.

How do you move inside a summer's day?
Like a hummingbird and a warrior,
like a woman in her best skirt
when she knows men are watching,
and she holds everything still,
deep, for one long moment
before she turns and looks back
and the world moves
into familiar places again.

more than once a bird of prey

more than once a bird of prey
has splintered by his feet

he can never sharply kill
instead cradles it rustling up from the ground and weighs
on his flesh the carrion stench
the basket strawness   the low clucking breath

the bird does not flap or crow but glares brazen
while he probes a severed talon
a hanging wing   a torn breast   then presses
the wild into his own warmth and the bird miraculously sleeps
within the hollow pump of his blood

it would be simpler to walk past
or crush the wounded with a stone to the head
but he believes they intercept his path as prayers
to prolong death
        with murmuring fingers and annointing voice
he does and each time he bends to gather
another fierce life in the grasp   it seems
he raises something of himself
though each time he stoops
again he buries it fresh

and sometimes then his grieving is so acute
I have to turn away

Prairie

The prairie is in early spring;
dirty blond stubble stretches on;
barely a tree grows:
a few black shrubs.
A sky more relentless than the land paints
a blue dome overhead and places me
at the centre. Looking, I think:
if the whole scene turned
the dirt would fall around me
like snow.

The road too is dirt with stones so large
I slow the car.
There has been no other traffic;
no one. Just cattle,
then dogs who bared their razor teeth
at my approach, and now
five white and tan antelope race
across the pale grass:
some other horizon.

I pass shacks collapsed,
skewed to one side.
I wonder why they were built;
why abandoned.
Even hawks wait from fence posts:
wind has pushed everything else to ground.
There are fences, yes, of rusted wire and decayed wood
staking limits so immense I cannot see
homes or barns;
such structures fall away from sight
as if they too have turned
to soil.

Quiet hangs in the air.
I hear it above the motor roar, above
the cassette beat, above
the wind drone through the open windows. It settles
like dirt over the interior of my car.
Through the windshield a distant line
joins prairie to sky. At its centre
the narrow road tries to cross.
I slow down further
and strain forward to see

a single cowboy
on his horse herding cattle
from one patch of land to another.
With an arm sleeved and buttoned against the sun
he raises his hat in greeting.
In the mirror I watch
a plume of dust obscure his face,
his hat cutting an arc of gray
across the blue.

*

For months now these pictures cling
like thunderstorms which threaten but will not break.
Looking, I think:
things are vectors positioned, spaced, and connected;
I spend entire days drawing lines.

Tightrope Walking

The night is stretched across my headache
I am balancing the pain. Did you say
something? It was only about your father's
illness. The compulsive photographs you took
covering the decay with black and white hard
cold lens. I am cutting up the negatives

now, preparing the paper for its ultimate map.
His body laid out in the developing pans. I
wonder as I mix the chemicals and fill the bath
with acid, where you are in all this, perhaps
cut away, I will find you later as I sweep,

excess discarded on the floor. We can put together
the story of your life, the hours emptied on
the couch beside your father's sickbed, the words
you have never showed me, your mother's soft
and constant reminders of rain as she cries in

the next room. Such musings are what I hang out
to dry as the photos come to light. The birth
of your father is slow and I can hear very clearly
the each tick of his heart. I am waiting for
the photos to show your shadow taking the picture
before the body is complete.

A Different Season

Walking in the park, you remember
another morning in a different season,
your mother, tottering, half cut from early
morning rye, your son just turned sixteen,
surly and rebellious, their war a bitter
rose you clench between your teeth —
you bite down hard, attempt forgiveness.
You take his part, she accuses.

You remember the mallards, their crests,
green and luminous, the morning glinting
in the water & you believe if you close
your eyes you might fall into this green,
escape into the mutability of the trees.
You recreate worlds; seek redemption
in a different season. But this is impossible,
the drama that plays before you like a slow
motion flick cannot be turned off, it plays
& replays, long after the death of your mother,
your son grown into tenderness.

In the scene you return to, the foreground is bloody;
rose petals fall in a drunken heap. You try to pick
a blossom, but the vine is green, refuses
to break. The rose hangs limply. Your mother
rages at your son. He tells her he's had enough,
calls her old and crazy, crazy, refuses to dance
to anything but joy. You can induce no guilt from
him. You capture her eyes, framed against
the morning in a thousand useless epiphanies.

She will leave the next day, and this final
moment, will whirl before you again and again,
each frame slipping into its own vertiginous
place, shifting in your memory like glass in
a kaleidoscope. You press the barrel against
your eye. The colours are capricious.
Her last two months spent in distant parks.
No sullen grandson. No silent daughter.
Only the purity of loneliness and sky.

SOPHIA LECKER

We Prayed For No Reason

Objects seem older at midnight. Books,
folded glasses,
the bas-relief of the cup on my table
are tranquil in the half-moon
cast by the lamp.
These things are somehow like a city
the people will abandon
when I turn off the light.
Structures are smaller now
more intimate
after so many years of unthinking usage —
Worn sun dials,
inscriptions, a temple
where people prayed
to a deity
whose name no one now remembers.
But I do remember
because they are all my own invention.
It feels lonely,
having so much history in my mind.
        I turn off the light. The author
disappears into the night.
Outside, snow falls,
covering the heavy grooves of wheels
even the bootprints of giants
so the likes of us
will surely be forgotten.
Only a few words
dim haloes of our grateful gestures,
the small fossils of the things
we didn't know we cherished
may remain. You who come after us
remember
we prayed for no reason
we sang in the night

Gin Wave

after three nights like this
   spinning on Jarvis St.
      poor wet Jarvis St. trying to wash
   my head away   my head is way
is teetering
  shoulder-high   is   head is
      dripping sky   drifting on my
         lemon wave lemon gin waving   on Valium
            waving for cars to slow   come in
            slow like the tide
can't quite make out
   their watery faces out
      through my seaweed lashes
         just little   just a little further
            just couple more pirates   irates
            sinking because
               slinking below sea level
                  dragging hooks   opening my
                  dragging off my cold ocean flesh
            a little more   few more pearls
         and I can steal backmybaby   backmy
            babies all the babies and swimandfly and fly
         to the warm brown sand

V. Symmetries of dilation

Early griefs lay down the shape —
as a baby nautilus creates
   with its first seed-chamber
   the opalescent model
     for its unfolding
     growth.

Death of a pet turtle. Its small life taken
for granted. But, in the ritual —
   for pastel roses cut from birthday cards
   and pasted on a cardboard box, the hollow
     dug with a spoon from the kitchen drawer —
     sadness swallows us.
We feel again the scrabble of minute claws
against our palm, remember the sideways
   scoop of stubby legs. In wrapping
   the shallow-domed shell with pink tissue,
     we come to know completely
     that the narrow head will never
emerge again. Remember our delight?
that first time, when we saw the cords
   stretch beneath the pleated skin
   and the miniature jaws
     open.

The newer griefs grow larger, but
no different in shape. The great griefs
loom ahead. Their mouths open wider
   and wider, create
   the laminate structure of loss —
   sea creatures building a universe
     of spiralled pearl. Hold that opening
     to your ear and listen
     to the empty
       palaces

Note: in mathematics, "symmetry" refers to the various kinds of transformation that leave something apparently unchanged.

DAVID O'MEARA

A Half-Remembered Year

Honestly, I don't know who ran
the machines this summer. The year began

stillborn in a frozen deadlock —
spring never came, we just rocked

and struggled in the frost, storefronts still
whimpering two weeks into April, until

over four sudden days, the city
simmered in a frying pan, humidity

gearing up into a stagnant damp.
We sweated and sweated, climbed the ramp

of summer's warehouse, and gathered the dry
stacks of our anger and sorrow inside

us. I don't know if I talked
to anyone. I can't imagine what

I could've said. But when the sun's doors
would open and dry off the coarse

gobs of dew, I raced to every
street corner, endlessly expecting to see

you when I stopped. I never did.
You'd already packed and slid

away to another continent, fair warning
and all. I'd been half-crazy trying

to track these tremors that bled
the voice of reason right out of my head

and gripped this life like I was
a stick to be pointed, but always

at you. It seems so simple: speak what
you feel, and everything else, just keep your trap shut.

But none of that meant anything to me.
Your smile was a shot of rye whisky,

and when you'd pour out that bucket of brown
dusty hair, I'd choke and feel about to drown.

I'll shape my heart, now that you've gone
to fit the sleeping echo of your bones.

There's only one leaf ...

There's only one leaf
lying on the wet pavement
    — and it's on fire

Tarpaper

I.

Look to the moon, they always said, or listen
    for the creek's unwaning spill of crescendo
        to fill your eyes and ears
in place of green leaves and the cricket's plainsong;
    they will sustain you through the year's
declining light and heat, and your own.

But the creek's words stick frozen in its throat;
    cold has stopped the wind's tin whistle;
        and the moon's no help: its round
idiot faces takes in the snow and floats
    trapped where, rivalling hardened ground
the wash of stars has set to dark blue marble.

II.

I have walked out tonight — called from my warm
    kitchen by black on the horizon,
        deeper than the streaked shoals
of sky that border it — to where the farm
    ends at half-buried, iced split rails.
Moonlight spills through them, shimmer of white neon,

but I can't take my eyes of that black well
    which, closer now, resolves into
        the north wall of a house —
derelict once, bought, half brought back from rubble
    by a handyman's devotion
whose soft slowness thwarts what his hands do.

III.

Last year he picked its withered crop of shingles,
    and on the bared, waterstained wood
        he tacked up tarpaper
in sheets, like sketching-paper on an easel
    propped behind a stack of cedar
he meant to face it with before the cold

set in. The stack, now taller by two feet
    of drift, matches corded hardwood
        heaped against the side
he did finish — a pale wall out of sight
    from here, where one coal-black facade
must stand for the whole house asleep behind it.

IV.

It is enough: although all fall its rawness
    pained like an unbandaged wound,
        tonight the wall prevails
against an enemy that has slung chains
    from eaves and porch, and turned handrails
to glistening treachery. Alone it stands,

black woodstove warming up the earth's cold kitchen
    with its soft, perishable skin
        of tar — preservative
whose power comes from its decomposition —
    in the inhuman dead of winter
standing for what's unfinished and alive.

Personations: 12

A fault runs through this mind full of ghostly fish
     that flicker food. What isn't meant to be
        a metaphor is more a kind of re-
Membering
          hunger.
In the teeth of it.
In the teeth of it cannot escape.
Can knot Occam's razor & Davey Jones' Locker
     with the same sad detachment.
Sad, the way sunlight lends its sparkle
     & water sudden swells & breaking
Breaks
         dashing its progeny across the shore.
Christ, we say, for no particular reason.
Or Beluga, for jerky newsreel we seem to recollect.
Or the number of surrealists it takes to change a lightbulb
Is a joke.
As well, every spear learned to plunge six
     blind inches from the heart to secure a meal
        should make automatic & final.
Should.
Excepting these fish unbound by any bent light
Turn tail.
They

Flicker

First Day Away

These walls and berry brambles
have always kept the sheep from the world.
Only impossible thistles stand among them.
At the brow of the walk a kestrel
hangs on the passing air,

and here my young father, whom you never knew,
looked down toward the city in the mist
and thought of crossing to America.
Searching for a reason for myself,
I have left you there.

A brief dawn brightens green and fails
beneath a cold cloud quickly drawn.
My shutters catch the wind and close.
No matter. This cheap room, up two twisting flights
looks out on flagstones only, splashed by gutter-spouts,

and on a river high on rain,
meeting the Atlantic tide
at a line of foam,
first seam in that wind-woven gaberdine
flung against shores afire with fuchsia.

Sparrows fall on crusts of yesterday's baguette
eyeing magpies not too proud
to strut among them. An indifferent cat
scatters them chattering to trees
that have reached up into centuries.

At noon, the sun gleams wet on bankside
rowanberry. Derelict lilies and dry-fruited
honeysuckle line the towpath walls.
Soft-bosomed Cleopatras pass
on barges of mahogany and brass.

At dusk, I go down to the tired sea
for fish and chips. Flickering lights
make fantasies along the front.
But tramloads of insistent merrymakers
turn away for beer and bingo.

High clouds tighten over our horizons,
and darkness eases, deepens again
with tedious predictability.
No summer netaphors remain. The flat Atlantic
chills the hours of empty air between us.

Origins

1.

In another version
a panic-stricken Joseph banishes Mary to the desert
to escape her tyrant father
who might slaughter them both

she wanders among the Bedouins   veiled & anonymous
across the shifting dunes

on a clear night
the camels form a mystic circle around her
while she coughs the bloodwet child
through a slit in her body

names him Fady
like Jesus in Hebrew
bundles him in goat-hair & leaves
him on a barren woman's doorstep
limp & wrinkled   perfect animal
of her womb

begs a star in the East
to light her way back

2.

Miral gives birth during a ceasefire
weaves the infant in egg-shell blue
& chances the mountain
sky bright as a dime

suddenly
War splits the air

random specks & flying shapes
catching the windshield   heads tossed back
mouths agape

dust & wind in all directions
like confetti. She gropes for the pieces
of the car floor   sheltering the boy
in the large tent of her body

& fanfare
scatters the knoll

Bird Watching

Holds you, not
only for bird reasons, but
because it slows you
down enough, silences
you enough to show, so you know, what
the place where you stand
sounds like when
you are not there.

The Butterfly Festival

I heard that in Japan
there are butterfly festivals,
but wherever I visited
among bookstores and libraries
looking for accounts of them, I could find none.
With us, was it the wanting
to be as close as any two ever
that led us to emptiness?
I tell myself now what I know
in a small set of details:
the silent plea, indecipherable and unexplainable
even to yourself,
and the child's fear and anger
that could never find words,
and the crystalline, shadow-draped echo
that I continually dreamt of
through all the nights you lay beside me.
Whatever it was in you
that made your touch and gestures
delicately trace out panic
was for me the most unknown
and most familiar thing.
I hold you in that instant
of sudden stillness and wild surprise
when it is as if we have both just sipped
the same dewdrop of wine
and it is the end of the rite
and your swept, velvety, glittering glance
is a profusion of butterflies
opening black wings
and finally flying away.

Something whole

Sometimes I think I'm simple,
a single-celled animal,
semi-permeable membrane thick,
round as the rim on a bumper car.
Resilient, so it can pinball off experience.
And does, until that moment when something,
misery or happiness, ruptures.
Something whole happens
and I'm flooded with it.
Like the shock the tv gave,
shoved me across the room.
Or the long day, blue and white,
in the November snow of the mountains,
high above anything human, silent,
day I can still step into, any time,
the way I can take in the wind
that cut the girl who held the steel
of monkeybars to watch other
children play distantly below. Brief and sudden
as the arched back and dorsal fin
of the minke whale in the Saguenay
whose leap left a mirror of oil
and blackness, stillness,
on the water, it makes you simple,
unitary and solid, indivisible.
Makes you full, the way the wheat is full
when it's taken in sun
until its being is burnished gold. Full as
the hawk balancing the air,
the drunk balancing the street,
which may tip and, tipping,
draw the world with it.

CHRISTL VERDUYN

In the cemetery

my mother on a motorcycle pulling up in a cloud
of noise the motor her voice above singing
in her mothertongue in the cemetery where my father is

working and I playing waiting for him or for her to go home
she is bringing us something cool to drink a bottle of buttermilk
against an august sun

the grass my mother and I cross is dry hurts the feet my father
under his beach umbrella the one bright spot in a burnt-out plot
he is chiselling today working the stone the old fashioned way
how he can work at all is a wonder on this hot hot August day

at the very last moment my mother says hello he looks up spits
of sweat all over his face adjusts his umbrella against the sun
my mother asks is he thirsty she has brought cold buttermilk

pleased my father stands up beside my mother for a moment they
make a couple my mother holding out a cold carton my father
drinking buttermilk in a cemetery

December 6

— Fifth anniversary, Montreal massacre

Into the morning drizzle
and snowpatch to see the year's
second-highest tide. No.
To witness it. Familiar
weeds and beaches plunged
into unaccustomed salt. A gun-
metal sky. Along the shore
we make sure the boats are tied.
(An escaping boat always holds
a good story. The Boston
Whaler upside down off
Lund, the officer who phoned
afraid he was notifying
the bereaved.) We reach the logs
we spiked and roped last summer,
ganged at the back of the bay.
If logs could talk: the seed,
the coming-of-age, the time
in water. They float, speechless,
their stories shuttling into ours:
fenceposts around the new field,
roof-shakes, wide boards to sheath
a building. Till then they wait,
good children in a classroom.
Lay your heads on your desks.
I'll tell you fourteen stories.
Fifteen. There was no rescue
and no escape. The numbers
on the tide chart and calendar
summon us: *Witness it.*